Unit

Let's Make a Difference

Mc
Graw
Hill
Education

Contents

Detective Brown strode up to Sue
Sprout and stared. She stated, "I hear
that you have a big problem now."

"It's my string beans!" howled Sue
Sprout. "I'm out of string beans. They
have been taken! Should I blame
myself for not watching them?"

Detective Brown scratched her head and frowned. "Tell me about this problem so I can build a case. Do you know where the beans are?"

Sue Sprout said, "I came out to water my pretty beans just a few minutes ago. I saw that just one little green bean was here. How dare someone take my green beans. It's just not fair!"

Detective Brown wrote notes on her pad. "I don't know if your dad heard a loud sound," she said. Then she looked through her special glass and said, "Look, there are brown tracks that lead to the stream. They look like little hands, so we know it isn't a bear. Let's take a walk and see if the robber is there." So that's what they did.

At the stream Sue Spout shouted, "Look out for the mud!" But Detective Brown slipped, and her body hit the ground with a wet splash. But neither her coat nor hair got wet.

Detective Brown yelled, "I should be wearing my glasses, but I don't see any beans here."

At home, young Steve Sprout pushed his way outside. Dad came out of the house with a big, hot pot. Steve said, "Dad asked Detective Brown to stay right here for some string bean soup."

Detective Brown said, "Well, that is the answer we've been hoping to find. Now we know where the string beans went. Case closed!"

6

Let's Help Out!

You can help out in your town in so many ways. Use your head and you can find the answer to many problems!

How about helping out in the park?
You can pick up trash and sticks that
are on the ground. A big crowd of
helpers can do a big job. A clean park
means a lot to people in your town.

Fuse/Getty Images

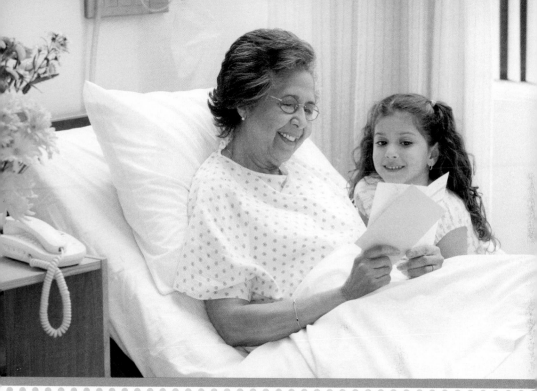

You can help out people in your town. If a neighbor is sick, a few minutes with that person means a lot. You might read to her or him. You might make a pretty get well card.

Does a neighbor need help when it snows? The town's snow plow can't take care of all the snow. You can help by clearing up the snowy paths to the house.

How can you help out in your town? There are many ways. Try just one!

Let's Join Joy's Show!

Joy tells the best jokes of any girl or boy in the class. No one can hear Joy's jokes without laughing.

Just last week Joy was with several friends. The group was busy having a good time. Joy brought her best jokes to tell. The kids liked her joke about a little toy rattle the best.

"I don't want to spoil a good time," Joy said, "but I want to plan a talent show! I can tell jokes, Troy can sing, and maybe Jen can play the drums."

The kids all started to speak at the same time. It was so noisy!

"Please be quiet," Joy shouted. "Who else would like to be in the show? I'll write down your name and make a list of the acts."

Troy and I put up signs, and lots of kids asked to join the show. Mr. Floyd said that he would love to help.

On the day of the show, it rained, and the wind blew. When it was time to start, Joy and her family weren't there! Jen played the drums, Troy sang, but still Joy did not show up!

Her friends were not happy.

"Joy! Joy! We want Joy's jokes now!"
the kids yelled.

"Where is she?" Mr. Floyd frowned.

Then a boy pointed at the door.
There stood Joy! She dripped with rain,
but she was all set to make us laugh!
The crowd cheered her on.

Boy, did the kids laugh and make
noise at Joy's jokes! Mr. Floyd and the
crowd clapped loudly.

The show was a big hit because of
Joy. All the kids had fun and were proud
to be up on stage.

Next year Joy will plan another talent
show, but she will not be late!

Join a Team!

One way to find out how to work together is to join a sports team. You can stay busy and feel happy!

A girl joined a soccer team. She made new friends and found out how to play a new sport. She found out how to pass to other kids and score points. She found out how to be a good teammate.

Her mom brought oranges to the game. The girls loved the sweet treat!

Blend Images - Erik Isakson/Brand X Pictures/Getty Images

This boy joined a basketball team. He met a lot of boys he liked. He found out that this game is a team sport, too. From the first coin toss that starts a game, players play hard to score points. They foil the other team's plays. One player can't do it all. Winning is a joint effort.

19

Softball is a team sport, too. A pitcher needs other players to help him or her win. The short stop catches ground balls. Other players catch fly balls. When you bat, your teammates cheer and make noise for you. That's part of being a team!

Soon the North Wind Blew

One day the North Wind and the Sun talked about which was stronger.

"Don't be a rude," said the Wind. "Did you forget about the time I blew off that roof during a storm?" he asked. "I can destroy with my might. It is true. I have always been stronger than you."

"But did you ever hear about the time I dried up all the water to make that desert?" said the Sun. "That is a clue to how strong I am. I couldn't have done that unless I was very strong. You shouldn't forget that."

This went on morning, noon, and night. The Moon grew sick of their cruel bickering.

"It is my duty to stop
this. I have a plan," said the Moon.

The Moon was wise, so the Wind
and the Sun said they would let her
draw up a plan.

"Here are the rules. The stronger
of you will get that man walking
along in his suit to take off his coat
using nothing but your own might.
That will be the proof we truly
need." said Moon.

The North Wind went first. He blew a strong, noisy wind. It was so strong that fruit blew off the fruit trees, which made him full of joy. But that just meant that the man grasped his coat tighter and wouldn't take it off. The man felt too cool to get rid of his warm coat.

Next, the Sun shone down on the man. Soon the man was oozing with heat and sat down to rest. He took a rock out of his shoe and then walked on. The man was sweating from head to toe as the strong sun beat down on him. Soon he was so hot that he threw off his coat.

"Well," said the Moon, "I watched the whole thing. I conclude that we have a winner. The Sun is stronger than the North Wind."

The North Wind was in a bad mood. Only one thing would make him feel better. He needed to blow off some steam.

The wind took in a
few deep gulps of air and blew
with all his might. He blew until the
man's coat blew right out of sight!
Now the man could not put his coat
back on even if he wanted to.

And that is the end of the story
about the Sun and the North Wind.

It Couldn't Be Done!

People have always said, "It couldn't be done!" Let's look at people that showed it could be true. They wanted to change the rules.

Could we fly to the moon or live in space? Some people said that it couldn't ever be done. Yet it did! In 1969, astronauts landed on the moon.

Now astronauts can stay in space for a long time. They take dried and fresh foods like fruit with them.

Alexander Graham Bell

Could we speak to someone far away? People said that it couldn't be done. Thanks to a man named Alexander Graham Bell, now we can.

The phone enabled us to speak to others in many places. Now, we can even use a cell phone in the park, in the woods, or on a ship!

Charles Jenkins

Could you watch a sports game without being there? "It couldn't be done!" people said.

Thanks to a man named Charles Jenkins, now we have the joy of watching TV. We can watch sports, news, shows, and a lot more. We even put on the TV when we have the flu!

Paul Saw
Arctic Foxes

Paul yawned and crawled out of
bed at dawn. It was only five o'clock
in the morning. Paul ate fruit and
toast till he was full. He drank warm
tea, too. He knew it was cold outside.

Paul suited up to go out. Then
he caught sight of his new camera
and put it on his arm. He walked
out into the cold, treeless land as
the wind blew.

When Paul was a boy, he saw a few TV shows about Arctic foxes. That launched Paul's study of the foxes. He had a lot of questions about them. He was always searching to find true facts about Arctic foxes. He read every book he saw about them.

As a grown man, Paul liked his job. He studied animals and took pictures of them in the wild.

It was spring, though it felt more like fall or winter because it was cold and raw outside. Paul's job taught him that Arctic days might be fine or awful. He sought a place where he could sit and watch for foxes.

Paul had good luck. He glanced down and saw what he was looking for—Arctic foxes and their cubs.

The mother fox watched her small cubs eat. The father fox had caught food for them. The cute cubs chewed on a huge piece of meat.

Paul could not know for sure, but he thought the foxes were 20 feet away. He hauled out his camera and took a picture.

The little foxes yawned and looked sleepy. Soon they would crawl back into their own den.

It was time for Paul to go to his home in the city. He had pictures to print! Those pictures would give clues about the life of the Arctic foxes. Paul would talk and write about them to teach others.

Small Ways to Save the Earth

"I can't save the Earth!" you might say. Maybe not, but if we all do a few small things, we can help a lot. Just give it some thought!

Be sure to turn off the lights or the TV when you are not in a room. Turn off the water spout when you brush your teeth. These are all small things you can do.

Ask your mother or father to put up a line for laundry on the lawn, or outside the window. The wind and sun will dry out the pants, shirts, sheets, and dresses.

It costs a lot to run a dryer. Why use it when you can dry things outside?

You can help out on Earth Day, too. On this day, people get together and clean their city or town. They put trash in bags, and a truck hauls it away the next day. Earth Day is fun! You can help and talk to friends at the same time. Share what you have been taught!

Don't
Dread
Rules!

Do you dread rules? You shouldn't fear them. All of us have to follow rules. Rules are a bit like laws. Pause and think about why people make rules.

We are taught rules to keep us safe. With rules, we stay out of trouble at school. Moms and dads ought to follow rules, too. Rules at work help workers treat each other fairly.

Fancy Collection/SuperStock

When you head off to school in the morning, you follow rules. You may walk or take a bus. On the bus you can talk, but rules say that you can't raise your voice. You also have to sit in a seat instead of standing up. Even if you brought a snack or lunch in your backpack, you can't eat it on the bus.

Once you get to school, there are more rules to follow. Children can't run in the halls or call out bad words.

In class, you raise your hand to talk about a book or paper you have read. This helps other kids learn.

Good manners count, too. Put your hand over your mouth when you sneeze or yawn so you don't spread germs.

Some schools have a rule that everybody in gym class must wear special shoes so they don't fall. Some kids have a whole uniform they wear in gym class.

When you play games like soccer, there are rules you should know so both teams play fairly. In soccer, you can hit the ball with your head, but you can't touch it with your hands.

This woman works on the schoolyard. She makes sure children follow the rules at recess. Rules help children stay safe.

One rule is that you should take turns. You should also share. If you are caught breaking a rule, you may get a warning. Then you will be more careful next time.

BananaStock/PunchStock

You have rules at home, too. Your family may have rules about doing chores, having friends over, and getting ready for bed. You also follow rules when you play games together.

It's good to talk with your mom and dad about rules they want you to follow. Make sure you understand them.

Rules help keep people in your town safe as well. If you're a smart person, you follow the rules.

When you're going for a bicycle ride, a good rule is to wear a helmet. When you're going for a car ride, a good rule is to wear a seatbelt.

So, be cool at home and school— don't break a single rule!

Stay Out of Trouble!

"Rules are good!" my mom and dad
said in a stern voice. "Follow them and
stay out of trouble."

What do they know? Children and young people get into trouble. It's what we do!

That day I ran down the hall on the way to the gym. I bumped into a friend, and she didn't like it. So my number one rule is "Walk down the hall." OK, I get that.

Before lunch, I broke in the line. My teacher saw me and made me go to the end. I was last into the lunchroom.

OK, so I found rule number two. It is "Stay in my place in line." It's just better to follow this rule.

At the pool, I walked too fast. I slipped and fell into the water. I was lucky I didn't hit my head! So rule number three is "Always walk slowly near the pool."

Now, I know that my mom and dad were right. Instead of breaking rules, I will follow them. Who knows? I might stay out of trouble!

Out of String Beans!

DECODABLE WORDS

Target Phonics Elements
 Diphthongs: *ou**: about, ground, house, loud, out, outside, shouted, sound, Sprout; *ow**: Brown, frowned, how, howled, now

HIGH-FREQUENCY WORDS

answer, been, body, build, head, heard, minutes, myself, pretty, pushed
Review: any, are, for, have, little, look, neither, of, one, problem, said, saw, should, some, special, through, to, walk, was, water, what, young, your
Story Words: detective, someone, soup

Let's Help Out!

DECODABLE WORDS

Target Phonics Elements
 Diphthongs: *ou**: about, ground, house; *ow**: plow, crowd, how, town

HIGH-FREQUENCY WORDS

pretty, minutes, head
Review: all, are, do, does, of, one, many, people, to, you
Story Words: neighbor, person

Let's Join Joy's Show

DECODABLE WORDS

Target Phonics Elements
 Diphthongs: *oy**: boy, Floyd, Joy, Joy's, toy, Troy; *oi**: join, noisy, pointed, spoil

HIGH-FREQUENCY WORDS

brought, busy, else, happy, I'll, laugh, love, maybe, please, several
Review: all, another, any, because, family, friends, good, group, have, help, of, one, put, said, stood, to, want, was, were, would, your
Story Words: door, quiet, talent, who

Join a Team!

DECODABLE WORDS

Target Phonics Elements
 Diphthongs: *oi**: join, joint, points, noise, coin, foil; *oy**: boy

HIGH-FREQUENCY WORDS

brought, busy, love, happy
Review: all, do, find, good, of, one, oranges, other, to, together, too, they, you, your
Story Words: effort, basketball, soccer

*Previously Taught

DECODABLE WORDS
Target Phonics Elements
Variant Vowels: *oo**: cool, mood, Moon, noon, oozing, proof, roof, soon, too; *u**: duty, truly; *u_e**: conclude, rude, rules; *ew**: blew, few, grew, threw; *ue**: clue, cruel, true; *ui**: fruit, suit; *oo*: took; *ou:* could, couldn't, shouldn't, would, wouldn't; *u** put

HIGH-FREQUENCY WORDS
air, along, always, ever, meant, nothing, story, strong
Review: all, been, done, even, from, have, head, of, off, one, only, said, some, to, very, was, watched, you, your
Story Words: desert, shoe, sweating, whole

It Couldn't Be Done! | WORD COUNT: 162

DECODABLE WORDS
Target Phonics Elements
Variant Vowels: *oo**: moon; *u**: flu; *oo*: look, woods; *ui**: fruit; *ew**: news; *ou:* couldn't; *u**: put

HIGH-FREQUENCY WORDS
ever, meant, always
Review: done, of, have, many, long, live, many, people, some, someone, to
Story Words: phone, astronauts, Jenkins, Alexander

DECODABLE WORDS
Target Phonics Elements
Variant Vowels; *a**: fall, small; *aw**: awful, crawl, crawled, dawn, raw, saw, yawned; *au**: hauled, launched, Paul, Paul's; *augh**: caught, taught; *al**: talk, walked; *ough:* sought, thought

HIGH-FREQUENCY WORDS
city, father, mother, o'clock, own, questions, read, searching, sure, though
Review: about, always, animals, away, because, every, give, into, of, others, picture, their, to, too, was, what
Story Words: camera, studied, study

Previously Taught

Small Ways to Save the Earth

DECODABLE WORDS
Target Phonics Elements
  Variant Vowels: *au**: hauls, taught, laundry; *aw**: lawn; *al**: small, all, talk

HIGH-FREQUENCY WORDS
  city, father, mother, sure
  Review: are, friends, water, your, to, their, together, do, people
  Story Words: Earth, laundry

Week 5 | Don't Dread Rules

DECODABLE WORDS
Target Phonics Elements
  Short Vowel Digraphs: *ea**: head, instead, ready; *ou*: trouble; *y*: gym

HIGH-FREQUENCY WORDS
  children, everybody, instead, paper, person, voice, whole, woman, words
  Review: about, also, are, do, even, family, friends, learn, of, once, other, over, people, school, some, special, sure, there, to, together, understand, want, you, your
  Story Words: shoes, uniform, bicycle, warning

Stay Out of Trouble!

DECODABLE WORDS
Target Phonics Elements
  Short Vowel Digraphs: *ea**: instead, head; *ou*: trouble, young; *y*: gym

HIGH-FREQUENCY WORDS
  children, instead, voice
  Review: are, friend, of, water, said, do, what, they, people, before, to, better, always
  Story Words: breaking, number

Previously Taught

57

HIGH FREQUENCY WORDS

Grade K

a
and
are
can
come
do
does
for
go
good
has
have
he
help
here
I
is
like
little
look
me
my
of
play
said
see
she
the
they
this
to
too
want
was
we
what
where
who
with
you

answer
any
around
away
be
been
before
began
better
blue
boy
brother
brought
build
busy
buy
by
call
carry
caught
children
climb
color
come
could
day
does
done
door
down
early
eat
eight
enough
every
eyes
fall
father
favorite
few
find
flew
food
found
four
friend
from
front
full
fun
girl

give
gone
good
great
green
grow
guess
happy
hard
heard
help
her
how
instead
into
jump
knew
know
large
laugh
learn
listen
live
love
make
many
money
month
more
mother
move
near
new
no
none
not
nothing
now
of
oh
old
once
one
only
or
other
our
out
over
people
picture

place
poor
pretty
pull
push
put
question
right
round
run
school
should
small
so
some
soon
start
sure
surprise
their
then
there
they
thought
three
through
today
together
tomorrow
too
toward
two
under
up
upon
very
use
walk
want
warm
water
way
were
what
who
why
woman
wonder
work
would
write

year
young
your

Grade 2

about
after
again
ago
air
all
almost
along
also
always
America
among
and
animal
another
answer
any
anything
apart
are
around
away
baby
ball
beautiful
because
been
before
began
begin
behind
below
better
bird
blue
body
both
bought
boy
brought
build
building
busy
buy
by
carry
certain
change
cheer

children
city
climbed
cold
colors
come
could
country
didn't
do
don't
done
down
draw
during
early
eat
eight
either
else
even
ever
every
everybody
everyone
eyes
fall
family
far
father
few
field
find
first
five
flower
food
for
found
friends
from
funny
girl
give
go
goes
gone
good
great
green
group
grow
happened
happy

has
have
he
head
hear
heard
heavy
help
here
house
how
hundred
hurt
I'll
idea
inside
instead
into
isn't
knew
know
laugh
learn
leaves
light
like
little
live
long
look
love
many
maybe
me
meant
minutes
more
morning
mother
move
my
myself
neither
never
new
nothing
now
number
o'clock
of
off
often
old
on

Grade I

about
above
after
again
ago
all
animal
another

once	places	searching	started	to	walk	won't
one	play	second	stood	today	want	words
only	please	see	story	together	warm	work
open	pretty	seven	straight	too	was	world
or	problem	several	strong	took	wash	would
orange	pull	she	sure	touch	watch	year
other	pushed	should	talk	toward	water	yellow
our	put	show	the	try	were	yes
out	questions	sky	their	turned	what	you
outside	read	sleep	there	two	where	young
over	ready	small	they	under	which	your
own	right	some	this	under-	who	
paper	said	Soon	those	stands	whole	
part	Saturday	sorry	though	until	why	
people	saw	sounds	thought	upon	without	
person	says	special	three	very	woman	
picture	school	start	through	voice	won	

DECODING SKILLS TAUGHT TO DATE

short *a, i; -s, -es* (plural nouns); short *e, o, u; -s, -es* (inflectional endings); two-letter blends: *r*-blends, *s*-blends, *t*-blends, *l*-blends; closed syllables; short *a*, long *a: a_e; -ed, -ing* (inflectional endings); short *i*, long *i: i_e;* possessives; short *o*, long *o: o_e;* short *u*, long *u: u_e; -ed, -ing* (w/ doubling final consonants; drop final *e*); CVC*e* syllables; soft *c* and *g; dge, ge, lge, nge, rge;* prefixes *re-, un-, dis-;* consonant digraphs *ch, -tch, sh, ph, th, ng, wh;* suffixes *-ful, -less;* three-letter blends: *scr, spr, str, thr, spl, shr;* compound words; long *a: a, ai, ay, ea, ei, eigh, ey;* contractions with *'s, 're, 'll, 've;* long *i: i, y, igh, ie;* open syllables; long *o: o, oa, ow, oe;* contractions with *not;* long *e: e, ee, ea, ie, y, ey, e_e; -s, -es* (change *y* to *i*); long *u: u_e, ew, ue, u;* comparative endings *-er, -est;* silent letters *wr, kn, gn, mb, sc;* prefixes/suffixes; *r*-controlled vowels *er, ir, ur, or;* inflectional endings; *r*-controlled vowels *or, ore, oar, ar;* plurals (irregular); *r*-controlled vowels *eer, ere, ear;* abbreviations; *r*-controlled vowels *are, air, ear, ere; r*-controlled vowel syllables; diphthongs *ou, ow;* plurals (irregular); diphthongs *oy, oi;* consonant + *le (el, al)* syllables; variant vowels *oo, u, u_e, ew, ue, ui;* contractions with *not (wouldn't, couldn't, shouldn't);* variant vowels: *a, aw, au, augh, al, ough;* vowel team syllables; short vowel digraphs *ea, ou, y;* alphabetical order (two letters)